Bitter Lemons

Lucy Hayes

methuen | drama

LONDON • NEW YORK • OXFORD • NEW DELHI • SYDNEY

METHUEN DRAMA
Bloomsbury Publishing Plc
50 Bedford Square, London, WC1B 3DP, UK
1385 Broadway, New York, NY 10018, USA
29 Earlsfort Terrace, Dublin 2, Ireland

BLOOMSBURY, METHUEN DRAMA and the Methuen
Drama logo are trademarks of Bloomsbury Publishing Plc

First published in Great Britain 2023

A catalogue record for this book is available from the British Library.

A catalog record for this book is available from the Library of Congress.

ISBN: PB: 978-1-3504-4167-5
ePDF: 978-1-3504-4168-2
eBook: 978-1-3504-4169-9

Series: Modern Plays

Typeset by Mark Heslington Ltd, Scarborough, North Yorkshire

To find out more about our authors and books visit
www.bloomsbury.com and sign up for our newsletters.

Bitter Lemons was first performed on 2 August 2023 at Pleasance Courtyard at the Edinburgh Festival Fringe and transferred to Bristol Old Vic in September 2023 with the following cast and creative team:

A – Chanel Waddock

B – Shannon Hayes

Director – Lucy Hayes

Designer – Roisin Martindale

Lighting Designer – Holly Ellis

Sound Designer – Hattie North

Additional Direction – Sara Aniqah Malik

Stage Manager – Han Sayles

Producer – RJG Productions

Chanel Waddock – A – she/her

Chanel trained at Bristol Old Vic Theatre School (2020 Graduate). Theatre credits include *Othello* (Frantic Assembly), *Rock/Paper/Scissors* (Sheffield Crucible), *Hamlet* (National Theatre), *Bonsai Baby* (Theatre503) and *We Need to Talk About Grief* R&D (Donmar Warehouse). Television credits include *Andor* S2 (Disney+), *Sneakerhead* (Steve Monger/Roughcut/Dave), *London Kills* (BBC/Acorn) and *This Is Going to Hurt* (BBC/Sister Pictures). Awards: Ian Charleson Award 2023 nominee for Desdemona in Frantic Assembly's *Othello*. Agent: The Artists Partnership (Alice Coles).

Shannon Hayes – B – she/her

Shannon graduated from Oxford University before going on to study at Bristol Old Vic Theatre School. Theatre credits include *Raya* (Hampstead Theatre Downstairs), *The Ridiculous Darkness* (Gate Theatre) and *Seven Pomegranate Seeds* (Rose Theatre). TV credits include *Vigil* Season 2 (BBC One), *Ted Lasso* (Apple TV), *I Hate Suzie* S2 (Sky TV), *Years and Years* (BBC One) and *Undercover* (BBC One).

Lucy Hayes – she/her – Writer and Director

Lucy is a writer and director from east London. Credits as writer include *Bonsai Baby* (Theatre503) and *But Still Michael Grew* (BBC Radio Bristol). Credits as director include *Plant Daddy* (Pleasance), *Hedda* (Oxford Playhouse) and *The Wind Blows Free* (Tristan Bates Theatre). Credits as assistant/associate director include *Macbeth* (Shakespeare's Globe), *Raya* (Hampstead Theatre) and *Le Malade Imaginaire* (Festival de théâtre de Richelieu). She trained at the University of Oxford and Bristol Old Vic Theatre School, and is a supported writer with Hampstead Theatre's Inspire programme.

Roisin Martindale – she/they – Designer

Roisin graduated in 2019 with an MA in Performance Design from Bristol Old Vic Theatre School and now works as a set and costume designer based in south London. Design work includes *Phantasmagoria* (Kali Theatre – UK tour), *I am England*, *Blood Wedding*, *The Wardrobe/It Snows* (all Egg Theatre, Bath), *Never Not Once* (Park Theatre 90) and *New Beginnings* (Kiln Theatre Youth Programme). Assistant/associate work includes *Disruption* (Park Theatre 200), *Sweeney Todd* (Egg Theatre, Bath) and *Big Big Sky* (Hampstead Theatre). Exhibition work includes *Hallyu! The Korean Wave* (V&A). Roisin has worked on new writing development with Half Moon Children's Theatre and Weighed In Productions.

Holly Ellis – she/her – Lighting Designer

Holly's work includes *Spy for Spy* (Riverside Studios), *Blanket Ban* (Southwark Playhouse), *On the Ropes* (Park Theatre), *A Sherlock Carol* (Associate LD, Marylebone Theatre), *CASTEing* (Roundabout), *The Tempest* (Royal Central School of Speech and Drama), *Autopilot* (Pleasance Edinburgh), *Animal Kingdom* (Hampstead Theatre Downstairs), *Instructions for a Teenage Armageddon* (Southwark Playhouse – Offie nomination for Best Lighting Design), *All the Conversations and Another F***ing Play About* Race (Arts Ed), *Bobby and Amy* (North Wall/UK tour/Pleasance Edinburgh) and *Tokyo Rose* (Southwark Playhouse/UK tour) and *Errol's Garden* (UK tour). Please check out her website at *www.hollyellislighting.com*

Hattie North – she/her – Sound Designer

Hattie is a sound designer from Leeds. She studied at LAMDA and graduated with a BA in Production Arts. Recent work includes *Mumsy* (Hulltruck Theatre), *I Hate It Here* (Pleasance) and *The Borrowers* (Theatre by the Lake). Associate work includes *How Not to Drown* (Theatre Royal

Stratford East), *Mansfield Park* (Watermill Theatre) and *A Midsummer Night's Dream* (Stafford Gatehouse).

Sara Aniqah Malik – she/her – Additional Direction

Sara makes political new work. She was the resident assistant director at the Donmar Warehouse 2020–2022 and is an associate artist at Watermill Theatre. She was a recipient of the Michael Grandage Award 2019. She trained at Bristol Old Vic Theatre School. Credits as director include *The Last Days of Judas Iscariot* (ArtsEd), *Mosquitoes* (LAMDA), *A Midsummer Night's Dream* (Actors' Church), *Pity* (LAMDA), *Salaam* (VAULT Festival). Credits as associate director include *Tammy Faye* (Almeida Theatre), *The 47th* (Old Vic), *Force Majeure*, *Love and Other Acts of Violence*, *Blindness* (Donmar Warehouse), *Constellations* and *Walden* (West End).

Han Sayles – they/them – Stage Manager

Han is an Offie Award-nominated technical designer and stage manager based in London. Known for their 'atmospheric and striking' designs, Han has collaborated with drama, comedy, drag and cabaret productions across the UK. They most recently designed both lighting and video for the acclaimed *Perverts* at the King's Head Theatre. Han also worked as a technical stage manager on *30 and Out*, with successful runs in Brighton, Manchester and London. In addition, Han served as head of lighting and technical for London's inaugural AI Festival hosted by Omnibus Theatre, illuminating theatremakers innovating at the intersection of artificial intelligence and the arts. They are currently immersed in pre-production for *M U S I C* as both lighting and sound designer, set to land at the Pleasance this Edinburgh Fringe.

RJG Productions – Producer

RJG Productions is a theatre production company focusing on new writing. The company is currently producing *It's Headed Straight Towards Us* (Park Theatre), *Polko* (Paines Plough), *Bitter Lemons* (Pleasance & Bristol Old Vic) and *Earshot* with Hot Coals Productions (UK tour). Other credits include *Brilliant Jerks* by Joseph Charlton (Southwark Playhouse), *Amélie the Musical* (Criterion Theatre, West End), award-winning *A Hundred Words for Snow* by Tatty Hennessy (Trafalgar Studios, UK Tour & VAULT Festival) and the original production of *Anna X* by Joseph Charlton. Projects in development include *Attrition* by Tatty Hennessy, a commission as part of the Writers' Guild of Great Britain New Play Commission Scheme.

Twitter – @RJGProductions

Instagram – @rjgproductions

Facebook – @RJGProductions

Website – rjgproductions.co.uk

Bitter Lemons is supported by the Edinburgh National Partnership Award with Bristol Old Vic and Pleasance.

BRISTOL OLD VIC

Bristol Old Vic is the UK's longest continuously running theatre and has welcomed millions of people through its doors since opening nearly 260 years ago.

Led by Executive Director Charlotte Geeves and Artistic Director Nancy Medina, the organisation is committed to platforming and creating opportunities for the multitude of stories that Bristol and the UK have to offer.

From its extensively redeveloped building in the Old City, Bristol Old Vic offers a year-round programme of inspiring, original new work; one of UK theatre's biggest learning and engagement programmes; and one of the UK's leading artist development programmes. Plus, through Bristol Old Vic On Screen, audiences across the world have seen its productions live or on demand, including most recently Complicite's acclaimed *Drive Your Plow Over the Bones of the Dead* and its own stylish hit *Hamlet* – which was also shown in 250 cinemas across the UK.

'We will make a theatre which is for our whole community. Not a passive place but one of activism. Not one voice but many. We will ask questions of ourselves and of Bristol. We invite you to come on in and help us make this building sing with possibility.' *Nancy Medina, Artistic Director*

·PLEASANCE·

www.pleasance.co.uk

PLEASANCE THEATRE TRUST

The Pleasance has been at the heart of Fringe theatre and comedy since 1985. With an international profile and a network of alumni that reads like a Who's Who of contemporary comedy, drama and entertainment, the Pleasance is a place for the experimental and the new.

We're proud to be one of the most highly respected theatre venues at the Edinburgh Festival Fringe and in London. We welcome audiences in their hundreds of thousands. We are where performers, writers, directors, technicians, producers and the rest of the artistic community can develop ideas and feel fully supported.

The Pleasance is both a Festival Organisation of 27 temporary venues across three sites, and a London theatre and development centre, with two permanent performance spaces which operate year-round. The Pleasance in London and Edinburgh are entirely symbiotic. We're been a registered charity since 1995 in England and Wales and 2012 in Scotland, supporting opportunities for artists year round.

Acknowledgements

I'd like to thank the following people who helped *Bitter Lemons* on its journey: Ben and Tan at Bristol Old Vic, Jonny and the rest of the Pleasance team, the team at Masterclass, Francesca Amewudah-Rivers, Georgie Bailey, Carly Brownbridge, Jennifer Davis, Charlotte East, Saskia Laroque and Bea Wilson.

And of course I will be forever indebted to my wonderful cast and creative team: Shannon, Chanel, Sara, Rebecca, Roisin, Holly, Hattie and Han.

Author's Note

I wrote this play in September 2022, after the worst summer of my life. I was working in France, stuck in 45-degree heat, on a production that was falling apart, a long way from home. I'd struggled with French culture more than I expected – micro-aggressions were rife and were dismissed as nothing more than a cultural differences. I'd found it hard to articulate myself in a way that had been meaningful or challenging enough to views and ideas I found fundamentally cruel, and I felt like I'd failed.

In the year of the overturning of *Roe v. Wade*, I'd also been stunned by the stories of pregnancy and abortion that had happened to some of the nearest people to me – by their bravery, maturity and dignity in handling this incredibly complex and personal decision, by the behaviours of the men who had impregnated them and by the ignorance of a society who politicised them. Society unfolds invisibly around us every day, and by the time we have something tangible to disagree with, it is often too late.

The most striking detail I learnt in the researching of this play is that your pregnancy is dated from the date of your last period, not the date of conception. This is devastating for those facing abortion laws of six weeks in Alabama, Georgia, Idaho, Kentucky, Louisiana, Mississippi, Missouri, Ohio, Tennessee and Texas, as 'six' weeks, could be as little as three. If you find out you're pregnant because your period is late, this means you could have as little as four days to decide, book and travel for a termination. Our understanding of what early life looks like is more politically constructed than it is biologically accurate. In deciding what an unborn child's right to life was, Justice Alito, in the document leaked from the US Supreme Court, referenced the 'great authority' Matthew Hale, a seventeenth-century witchfinder, seventeen times.

One in three of us with uteruses will get an abortion in our lifetime. Yet many people do not think they even know someone who has had one, which only speaks to the culture of shame and silence that continues to surround this everyday reality for thousands of people. I've been amazed too by the complexity of the attitudes of those that would consider themselves pro-choice. Perhaps this is due to our moral anxieties around when life begins; about the potential for life, and our right to life at every stage of our existence. Yet a culture which continues to prioritise and exploit potential over the lived experience of everyday people are also the foundations of a capitalist, misogynistic, racist, homophobic and transphobic one. There is no potential there.

For the one in three

Bitter Lemons

When you lose control of your body,
you have just about lost all you have in this world
– Nancy White

A glassmaker is grinning
turning out new mirrors that lie
selling us
new clowns
– Audre Lorde

Characters

A, *mid-to-late twenties. White.*
B, *mid-to-late twenties. Mixed white and black heritage.*

Notes on the Play

The absence of punctuation is an invitation

The text has been 'scored' – the piece should be read across the page, left to right

A capital letter indicates a new sentence

Lines in italics are speech and it should be clear it is speech in delivery

A forward slash (/) indicates overlapping speech

One

A

You work in a man's job

.

.

You're a footballer
And a good one too

.

.

.

.

And in a few weeks you have a big match
You've been promoted to number one goalie
Your first time since you joined the club
A match that might finally prove that you deserve to be there

.

.

.

.

.

.

.

.

.

.

Remember when you were younger and you'd always get asked
What do you want to be when you grow up?
You said a footballer you want to be a footballer

B

You work in a man's job
You work in the city for a big fuck-off bank

.

.

You've been slowly climbing the ladder
Good grades good university good job

.

.

.

.

.

.

.

.

.

In a few weeks you have a big pitch
You've been chosen to lead the team
Even though you are the newest recruit
A pitch that might finally prove you deserve to be there
At least to yourself

.

.

.

.

.

.

.

.

.
.
.
.
.
.
.
.
And here you are
Your dreams came true
.
.
.
.
You don't know what you
expected it to feel like
But you didn't expect it to
feel like this
To feel so
.
.
.
.
Bruise and become bitter
Or
.
Realise
What did you
.

When you were younger you
were fed off dreams
Your mum did her best you
know she did but it was hard
on her own
But when you grow up she'd
say *you'll have a good job and a
good husband*
.
.
Here you are with a good
job
Not quite a husband but a
good boyfriend
.
.
.
.
.
As if your soul is
approaching an edge
And you don't know if you'll
bruise and take it
.
.
What sickness comes if you
.
.
What did you want

Two

A
It's the lead-up to the game
and you're getting ready for
another day of training
The Super League final

B
.
.
.
.

Interest in the women's
game has been growing since
the Lionesses won the Euros
and there's a feeling that this
one might finally be watched
Both by those who are there
for the game and by those
who still wonder
Can women really kick a ball
With their small feet and
inability to pretend to be
hurt when tackled
You've been in the same club
for years academy to
professional but you've
always been no. 2
Always waiting
Hoping
But the no. 1 goalie's been
there for years and there's
only one spot
And then last night you got
the call
Steph's off ACL rupture you're on
A call you'd be waiting for
your whole life
When you were younger you
used to get panic attacks
They started when you
began to hear your parents
arguing later and later into
the night
You'd feel the world falling
away around you
And you'd be falling not
being able to work out how
you might stop

How to slow down   .
How to save yourself   .
But then your dad gave you .
a ball   .
It was almost a joke at first .
Something for the two of   .
you to sneak off and do   .
while your dad pretended   .
he'd given up smoking   .
We won't tell your mum it'll be .
our thing our secret your dad .
would say   .
What she doesn't know can't .
hurt her   .
But then he realised you   .
were good   .
Looking good kid he'd shout as .
his cold fingers fumbled   .
round the end of a cigarette .
butt   .
And so he took you out to   .
play every Saturday   .
And he'd drive every week   .
to *a top-secret location* .
Even though it was the same .
place every time   .
That's why the journey to   .
practice is always your   .
favourite   .
You arrive at the training .
grounds and the morning   .
air dances over your face as .
you take in your home   .
The goal   .
24 feet wide and 8 feet deep .
192 square foot   .
And for the first time it's .
yours   .

Coach says there's a
philosophy behind good
goalkeeping
Predict the future
But don't anticipate it
When you defend the goal
you need to work out where
the ball might be coming from
See the direction of the pass
The angle of the body
The tilt of the foot
You watch
And then you act
As the ball soars through the
air
You position your body
Trying to slow down and
reposition time
Every shot that could have
been alive at once in your
body
Hundreds of versions of you
in thousands of places
The ball soars towards you
and
If you catch it
You're a soothsayer
You've managed to hold the
future in your hands
And you know what future
you want to hold
The Super League trophy
And a no. 1 shirt

Your favourite thing about
your job is arriving in the
morning
And this morning is no
different

You love how it's always cold
and crisp between the
skyscrapers the pavement
always in shade
The sun streams down and
you feel simultaneously like
you're below and on top of
the world
You strut through the
revolving glass door
Swish through the marble
reception the uniformity of
men in suits
You're wearing a fresh suit
with power shoulders
It's blue and when you put it
on you worried you looked a
bit like Thatcher
You asked your boyfriend
and he said maybe you did
But in a cool way
You're carrying a briefcase
even though you don't need
one
There's nothing in it but
lipstick and your birth
control
Everyone moves around you
like clockwork a perfectly
orchestrated display of
money and power
They look like they were
born to be here
And that's when your
briefcase starts to sweat
against your hand as if it
wants to leave

Even your lipstick grains
against your teeth as if it's
afraid to be caught on your
mouth
But you tell yourself your
mum is proud of you
And that your boyfriend is
too
Your mum adores your
boyfriend
He bought her flowers when
they first met
Sometimes you're surprised
that you're with him
He went to boarding school
And enjoyed it
But he is kind and reliable
and looks out for you and
you've not been used to that
Your mum did her best you
know she did but she
worked all the time and was
always trying to learn
Spanish
Although the only Spanish
she seems to know is *sangria*
and *uno mas*
You know it was hard for her
without your dad
Which is a generous term for
someone you've only met
once
You spent most of your
childhood worried about
money
You loved football but could
only do the free sessions so
your mum used to drive you

around sign you up to a new club each week until you ran out of options

Last year your mum got made redundant and called you embarrassed

She was getting behind on her mortgage payments

You said you'd help without thinking

But then a few months ago they put the rates up and the payments alongside your rent have put you into your overdraft

So you need to work as hard as you can to get a raise as soon as possible

You reapply your lipstick in the lift mirrors

It will be perfect

And so will you

Are you seeing anyone at the minute? Alex asks

You're in the changing room getting ready for warm-up

Sounds like you had a wild night with that barista

Have you seen him again?

Or the girl you went to school with? Who used to tease you and turned out she was a homo herself?

You're the tart of the football team

Football's always made you popular

Especially with the boys

You can see the relief in
men's eyes when they realise
they don't have to explain
the offside rule to you
Doesn't mean they still don't
The barista was your mum's
fault
A few weeks ago she told the
barista in your local coffee
shop that despite his new
heritage bean which is
sustainable and mindful of
the political and ethical
differences in South
America
She preferred instant
The barista looked taken
aback but you smoothed it
over
And on the way out you
noticed he'd written his
number on the inside of
your coffee cup
One thing led to another
and before you knew it you
were exploring your own
political and ethical
differences
Your mum's full of
controversial behaviours
She thinks cheese is a type of
salad
And that the only plumbers
you can trust are ones called
Keith
But you could never work
out why your mum didn't
like football

Isn't it a boy's game? she said   .
once   .
It's just very   .
Isn't it a bit   .
I don't know   .
Women running round after a   .
ball   .
She can't really understand   .
what you do as no. 2   .
How you can get paid to not   .
play   .
And how you could   .
complain   .
I'd love to get paid not to work   .
she'd reply   .
You head out to the pitch   .
annoyed by Alex's prying   .
You need to focus   .
Everything okay? coach   .
catches your shoulder as you   .
step onto the grass   .
We all want this to go well for   .
you   .
I know we all wish Steph a   .
speedy recovery but   .
It's time you stepped up   .
He slaps you on the back *no.*   .
1 goalie hey   .
You realise you've forgotten   .
your gloves   .
You've been doing so well since   .
– erm he says   .
Keep it together girl keep it   .
together   .
And remember the first principle   .
of goalkeeping   .
Predict the future   .
But don't anticipate it   .

I'm fine you say *great in fact*
Just need to get my gloves
.
.
.
.
.
.
.
.
.
.
.
.
.
.
.
.
.
.
.
.
.
.
.
.
.
.
.
.
.
.
.
.
.
.
.
.

.

.

You'll be a senior analyst by the time you're thirty your boss says to you in your morning meeting
You didn't sleep well and you can feel your tiredness jangling against your morning coffee but her comment makes you glow inside
The last good night's sleep you remember was in 2001
The night before your seventh birthday dreaming of the thick white icing you'd peel from your birthday cake
Sometimes in the night your boyfriend senses you're awake and reaches over to set up your headphones and latest audio book
You're here to talk about the pitch
And your boss is telling you this pitch is especially important as the company wants to attract new clients
Expand their range of investors make it more diverse
You wish the corporate world had never learnt that word because it feels more like a threat
She says the company is going through a financial

pinch and needs to grow
drastically if it's to stay
competitive

She asks *and how's your love
life?*

You hate it when she tries to
chat with you sister to sister
just because you're the only
women on the team which is
why you haven't told her
about your boyfriend

Last week she showed you
the tiny constellation of
bruises on her thigh

She's on her third round of
IVF

But she's optimistic she told
you

Her mum had kids too
young and was desperate
she wouldn't do the same

But if only she'd started
when she was your age she
could have had an army of
kids by now

You'd tried to avoid her eye
you don't want to talk about
kids

You know your boyfriend is
keen can't wait to have
children toddling around
with his eyes and last name

What about my name? you'd
said *they could have my last
name*

*But you don't even know your
dad* he'd said

And he didn't even know his

.
.
.
.
.
.
.
.
.
.
.
.
.
.
.
.
.

Predict the future
But don't anticipate it
It's a motto you've come to
live by
You grab your gloves and
see your phone vibrating
Mum? I'm in training I can't –
It's just a quick one she says
I heard them talking on the
radio what's it called the man
with the beard
Well I don't know if he's still got
a beard couldn't see him
But they said your name that
you're on that the other goalie's
injured
And Gina and Pete were talking
about it down the road
I told them I'm not really into it
but
How do I get a ticket?
The silence cracks in the
air

And you'd just stared as he
rubbed his signet ring
We have the same blood type was
all you managed to say as
you pushed down on the
plaster from your recent
blood donation grains of
plaster sticking to your
fingers
You dig your nails into your
skin
Everything okay? your boss
asks
I'm fine you shoot back *great*
in fact

.
.
.
.
.
.
.
.
.
.
.
.
.
.
.
.
.
.

You thought you'd misheard
her but she says it again
Your dad would have been there
I know he would have so
How do I get a ticket?
You've been waiting your
whole life for this but you
guess there's still things that
you can't predict
Your big game
A chance to prove yourself to
your coach and
To your mum

I wanted to talk to you about
something else your boss seems
cautious *we're having to do*
some rethinking
Streamlining the team trying to
make it more efficient which will
mean some losses
Your stomach plunges you
can't lose your job
But
We're also creating a new position
A Responsible Investment Lead
Someone to make sure we're
staying on track with our –
targets – ESG D&I what do you
think?
You're grateful you need it
but *I've taken an ESG*
introduction course but I've not
trained in D&I
Oh don't worry about it's very
straightforward
You'll be great at it
And the role will have all the
usual benefits

An office
A pay rise
And if the pitch goes well
She looks carefully at you
You feel your tiredness
vanish
You can get out of your
overdraft
Pay your mum's mortgage
maybe even pay it off
So
Her voice reaches out to you
catching you like a balloon
weight
You bring in those clients
And
It's yours
Up up up and away

Three

A

Before he died your dad
had called you up out of the
blue
And said make me proud in
a way that you knew carried
weight
After your parents' divorce
you didn't see him very
much
Weekends turned to
afternoons turned to *I'll catch
you next time*
But he always saw you in
a way your mum never
could

B

Always paid for your football
lessons
Every birthday an envelope
with another year's worth of
lessons and the same
message *Looking good kid*

And when you turned
professional you were
desperate to play a game so
you could invite him
He didn't tell anyone he had
cancer
Said he'd taken up running
and the weight had just
dropped off
But in just a few months
he'd gone
You'd got a call from an
unknown number three
months ago
A woman's voice at the end
of the phone that you didn't
recognise
I'm sorry she said *I'm so sorry*
as your skin plunged into ice
You'd sat on your bed and
stared into space until your
eyes were dry
The next morning put on
your boots and headed
straight to training
You didn't tell anyone
but you had to get coach's
permission to take the day
off for the funeral
And now you can feel his
eyes on you at all times

Which is exactly what you
didn't want to happen
*Keep it together girl keep it
together* he says to you every
morning
It's only been a few months
and you know that you're
doing fine
But recently you worry it's
catching up with you
because you feel shaky and
sick in the mornings
You even asked for extra
medicals blood tests urine
tests tests tests tests
But you suppose there's no
real test for heartbreak

Your head is swimming with
ideas as you leave your boss's
office
You'll research the clients
thoroughly
Get your boyfriend to help
he's great with charming
people
In the corridor you bump
into one of your colleagues
Gary
Who has a pink pencil
He keeps it in the top pocket
of his suit and the end pokes
out
A bright pink tip against
grey pinstripes like a badge
Gary joined the team before
you but only by a few
months
I was looking for you he says

.
.
.
.
.
.
.
.
.
.
.
.
.
.
.
.
.
.
.
.
.
.
.
.

I'd love a double shot
cappuccino with oat milk
You'd got Gary a coffee once
as a favour
Twice as a gesture of
goodwill
The third time you'd said
yes and then forgotten about
it and he'd shouted at you by
the printer
The fourth time you'd tried
to tell him it wasn't your job
But the fifth time you were
tired and wanted a caffeine
hit yourself
And that was over two years
ago
I'm a bit busy Gary you say to
him
I can go after lunch?
The thing is he says *the thing is*
is that I need some caffeine now
so it's going to be no good later
Okay you say *no worries*

Okay? Alex catches your arm
on the way back to the pitch
I'm sorry if that was a bit –
All good you say to Alex
Really trying to mean it
You love Alex but her whole
family comes to every match
They even come to practice
sometimes
Just to support
She lives in a world where
parents are proud of their
children no matter what

.
.
.
.
.
.
.
.
.
.
.

She doesn't understand how
important it is that your
mum likes the game
On the pitch coach blows his
whistle
Right everyone I know there's
been a lot of talk about next
season
Some of you might be looking to
transfer
Some of you might be looking to
step up
But we need to focus one game
at a time
And we not only need to win we
need to put on a good game
Show the skills we've been
learning show we're
developing the women's game
for our sponsors and channels
We've been working a long time
for this hype
So we're going to start with
training our new no. 1
Everyone turns to look at
you and your fear forces
itself into a smile
Line up
Penalties
Five minutes

Can I grab you for five minutes?
Your boss pops her head
from behind the door
I was just going to –
You can do that in a minute she
says
Come in
Take a seat

I think it would be good for you
to see this she says *for when*
you're calling the shots one day
You sit down and wonder
what's about to come
And then she pops her head
out again
Joe?
You don't process it at first
You just see a familiar mop
of sandy curls walk into the
room
Piercing blue eyes that catch
your own as he does a
double take to see you too
Come in your boss says again
Take a seat
And your boyfriend sits
down in front of you

The goal in front of you 24
feet wide and 8 feet deep
192 square foot
Coach is staring at you from
the stands
His eyes like two wounds in
your chest
Concentrate he shouts
Just like your dad used to
shout
You used to love those days
you two sneaking off
together before everything
changed
Don't tell Mum
You breathe in

You breathe out

You can feel the warmth of
your boss's thigh next to
you
The thigh of a thousand tiny
bruises
Thanks for coming in Joe your
boss is saying
He looks at you searching
your face what are you doing
here
You'd both agreed not to
mention you were dating to
anyone at work
He'd been your mentor
when you started
You'd shared a drunken
snog at work drinks
The next day you'd texted
him to say nothing could
happen
That you couldn't mix your
personal and professional
lives
He texted you back almost
immediately
Said to let him know when
you changed your mind
You'd never had a man be
present like that
Hoping
Waiting

Waiting one by one
Your team are lined up front
of you
It feels like you against the
world
Come at me bitch you want to
scream

You're a soothsayer
Predicting the future in
motion

You couldn't have predicted
any of it
How silly he is sometimes
How he loves football more
than he loves you
He's got tickets to a game
next week
For the women's team
They're quite good he said
they're actually quite good
You love football too and
he'd always teased you about
it tested your knowledge
But his silliness makes you
laugh
Like last night when you
were having sex and he was
convinced your boobs had
got bigger
So he got up and did a
celebration dance
And shouted *let's do it let's go*

Let go your coach is shouting
you're too tense
You'd like to see him *let go*
with five balls about to be
aimed at him
The first player takes her
aim
She's a lazy shooter she goes
back of the net to the left
every time
You could do this in your
sleep
She kicks and you dive

You hit the grass and stretch
out your hands
In the corner of your eye
you see the ball dribble to
the right

Right
Your boss starts talking
about the company's losses
versus expenditure
Efficacy restructuring the
headlines she's already said
to you
And then she says
So unfortunately
We're having to review the team
I'm sorry Joe
It's not personal
We've reviewed the figures from
the team and
We have to let you go
This can't be happening you
must have missed something

You've missed
You can't believe you've
missed
The second shooter lines up
You need to focus
Your mum is coming to the
game and you need to
perform
Even though football's
always been you and your
dad's thing
Don't tell Mum
Turns out that wasn't the
only thing he wasn't telling
Mum

Your football his cancer he
had a habit for keeping
secrets
One day your dad had taken
you to a new *top-secret location*
to train
Set you up to practise and
then said he just had to sort
something out
What he didn't know was
Your mum had followed
weary of the careful
conspiracy you both used to
carry
You'd been practising your
kick-ups when you first
heard the noise
Party music children's
chatter
And then the screaming
And you'd only seen a
glimpse of her before your
mum had forced you away
from your ball and into the
car
This other woman
Turns out what your mum
didn't know could hurt her
The next ball's flown past
you
I wasn't ready!

He's already stood up
Thanked your boss and
headed out to gather his
stuff by the time you come to
your senses
You run after him to see him
waiting by the lift

·
·
·
·
·
·
·
·
·
·
·
·
·
·
·
·
·
·
·
·
·

Coach is walking towards
you
*Give me another shot I won't
miss again*
But he blows his whistle

·

Everyone five minutes
Jones we need to talk
Penalties over

·

It's not fair you bark at coach
as soon as you get into his
office
I can do it you say *put me back
out there I can do it*
I'm your no. 1

Joe
He turns to look at you and
his gaze is so hurt you almost
wish he hadn't
I didn't know you tell him
He looks at you slowly
I didn't expect this from you
What?
*I didn't expect you of all people
to be comfortable with them – so
obviously playing the diversity
card*
*What? It was based on
performance it wasn't –*
*They never put my photo on the
website*
Yours was up on your first day
I'm good at my job
Yes
You are
And then he walks away

·
·
·
·
·

How is that fair?

·
·
·

How is any of this fair?

·
·
·
·
·
·

But he stands up gently and
opens the door behind you
to the medic
I'm sorry he says as he leaves
we can do penalties again later
Dr Jarrett wanted to see you
about your medical
Why don't you sit down?

.
.
.
.
.
.
.
.
.
.
.
.
.
.
.
.
.

You look down as your
phone buzzes
Half expecting it to be Gary
asking where his coffee is
But it's a call from blood
donation services
You pick up
Maybe it would feel good to
shout at someone
I donated blood a week ago if
you checked your records you
wouldn't be wasting my time
The man on the other end is
apologising it's not that
What you say *What do you*
want?

What? Your medical? Your
nausea
Is it possible that grief has
leaked into your body
Turned your tissue into
cabinets
Burying its baggage in your
blood bones and cavities
Transforming you donating
you

.
.
.
.
.
.
.
.
.

.
.
.
.

Sorry it's from the medical team
about your last donation
You immediately wish you
hadn't shouted at him

I'm sorry I've had a stressful day
No problem are you free to talk?
We've had something come back
from your sample

.

.

.

.

.

.

.

.

It's your urine sample the
medic says *it's come back and*
I've not taken anything you
shoot back
My antidepressants shouldn't
affect it although they've been
flagged before
But it's not that

.

.

Your urine contains
hormones
Hormones that normally
indicate

.

.

.

It's coming up positive on
the test

.

.

.

He's telling you that
That you're
Pregnant

They're calling to say your
blood contains abnormalities

.

.

.

.

It could be a multitude of
things you'll need to call
your GP for tests

.

.

But the first thing to check
for is
Because it might be that

.

That you're
Pregnant

Four

A

You've been sitting on the
floor for an hour

.

.

.

B

.

.

Pacing the office toilets with
your phone clutched to your
chest

Trying to work out if you
feel any different
.
.
.
Terrified that despite your
indecision your body has
already decided
So that's why you'd been
feeling sick
Not from the loss of your
dad
From the growth of a –
.
.
.
.
.
.
.
.
.
.
.
.
.
Are you sure you'd said to the
medic
It's not just a UTI?
You'd read about that once
No he'd said
Your urine contains the hormone
HCG
You're pregnant
Didn't you worry when you
missed your period?

.
.
Wondering how you can feel
exactly the same as an hour
ago
.
.
.
.
.
.
.
.
You'd picked up five
pregnancy tests at the
chemist and then panic
bought some polos
Acting as if that's what you
came in for and the tests
were an afterthought
You'd lined them up in a
row
Drunk a litre of orange
squash and peed on them
one after the other
Set your timer for three
minutes knowing it would
feel like an eternity
.
.
.
.
.
.
.
.
.
.

Not really you say
.
.
.
.
.
.
.
.
.
.
.
.
.
.

The fucking barista
With his fucking heritage
beans
You'd asked him to wear a
condom and he'd asked if
you could just get the
morning-after pill
And you should have said no
you know you should have
said no
But you were tired and sad
and fancied him a lot less
than you did two pints ago
The sex was average and
with a pace so platonic it felt
like you were walking
around Ikea
You know that hoping for
the best is not the most
reliable form of
contraception
But it's worked every time
you've had sex with men
before

.
You're looking at ten blue
lines
Every pregnancy test
betrayed you
But you don't understand
You'd been so careful
Sometimes you'd even make
him use a condom even
though you were on the
pill
Maybe it's just a UTI
You'd read about that
once
.
.
.
.
.
.
.
.
.
.
.
.
.
.
.
.
.
.
.
.
.

And maybe you knew deep
down when you missed your
period
But your dad had just died
and you thought you were
due some good karma

.

.

.

Do you know how many weeks?
You'd asked
Six weeks he'd said

.

You immediately try to find
out what that means
For your baby
You gag

.

You're not ready to say those
words yet

.

.

Your pregnancy at 1–12
weeks

.

Your pregnancy is dated from
the first day of your last period
Not the day that you had sex
Which means that during
the first two weeks of your
pregnancy you are not
actually pregnant

.

.

.

The inner layer will become
the lungs stomach gut and
bladder

.

.

.

.

.

.

You've also bought one of
those tests that tell you how
many weeks

.

.

.

Six weeks

.

.

.

.

You feel sick

.

.

On the NHS website you
find an article called
Your pregnancy at 1–12
weeks
At 1–3 weeks

.

.

.

.

.

.

At four weeks the embryo
has formed and splits into
three layers

.

.

.

.

.

.

The outer layer the brain and
nervous system eye lenses
tooth enamel skin and nails

.

.

The nervous system is
developing and foundations
for major organs are in place

.

.

Blood begins to circulate
around the blood vessels
that have formed

.

.

.

.

This will become the spine
brain and head
At six weeks

.

.

You read on
There's a large bulge where
the heart is
The embryo is curved and
has a tail and looks a bit like
a tadpole
The embryo is covered in a
thin layer of see-through
skin
The heart can sometimes be
seen beating at this stage
You're amazed at how this
person is becoming

The middle layer the heart
blood vessels muscles and
bones

.

.

.

At five weeks the embryo is
2 mm long

.

.

.

The heart is forming as a
simple tube-like structure

.

.

.

The outer layer of cells
develops a groove and folds
to form a hollow tube called
the neural tube

.

.

.

You pause
You can't read this yet

.

.

.

.

.

.

.

.

.

.

.

.

.

.

When you feel you've barely
become yourself

We've managed to find you a
consultation to talk about your
options the medic said
It's your choice of course
But with the game coming up we
thought that might be useful
We'll have to tell coach
It's his decision but it might be
best if you don't play
No
Please
Please don't tell him
I'll be fine I'll go to the
consultation

So your boyfriend had been
right about one thing in the
last twenty-four hours
Your boobs have got bigger
You're terrified to think
what would have happened
if you hadn't donated
blood
How many more weeks or
changes to your body before
it could even have been a
possibility

Dr Jarrett had been sceptical
but you kept insisting
This is my body no one else
should decide what it can and
can't do
I can play the game
Coach doesn't need to know
Tell him it was a UTI

You wonder if you should
tell your boyfriend

You wonder if you should
tell your mum
You gag
You wouldn't put it past her
to be pro-life

.

.

.

.

You get out your phone and
find your mum's number
It's 5 p.m. she'll just be
finishing work

.

.

.

.

.

.

.

.

.

.

.

.

.

.

.

.

Your finger hovers over her
number
Hi darling she'll say
She'll be quiet maybe even
sympathetic as you say
Mum I messed up

.

.

.

.

.

He wants kids
Maybe this would make
everything better between
you

.

.

.

.

Your boss knocks on the
door of the cubicle
You grab the tests and shove
them down your top
Everything okay in there?
Yep fine
You open the door trying to
appear as calm as possible
Women's issues you grimace
And in a grand gesture of
feminism your boss takes
your hand and squeezes
it
You can feel the urine from
the tests making small
patches on your shirt
I'm sorry she says *I didn't know*
you two were together
Bad move from me

.

.

.

.

.

.

And then she'll ask *and who is*
the father?
And you'll go quiet as you
struggle to remember his
name
And you'll feel sympathy
start to drain away as
judgement soaks in

On your way back to your
desk you can see
Gary staring at you and you
try to avoid his eye
He lays his head on the
desk
Sorry he pops up *just drifted*
off there
Not sure why I'm so tired should
have had a coffee

How did you get here
You look back through time
and feel stupid

I've got something I want to
show you
He jumps up
I've been working on these slides
for the pitch
On the first slide there's the
picture of you from the
website
What's your heritage? Gary
had said as he'd taken it
My mum's Nigerian and my
dad's mixed race you'd replied
automatically
Oh he'd said *that's funny you*
don't look mixed race
Can you pull your hair back it's
on your face?

You hadn't really replied just
tucked your hair behind
your ears and felt yet again
you weren't good enough
Gary scrolls to a graph on
the next slide and the
brightness of the lines swim
in your face
His breath smells like
frothed milk and roast pork
The lines of the graph
everywhere edges for you
to hit

You can't predict the future
Can't anticipate it
You're not in control of
anything
Not even your own body

Lines like
Cliffs for you to climb
Mountains for you to fall
off
And then
And then

But baby
You tried

You say
Looks great Gary
And swallow it all

Five

A
.

A few days later a taxi picks
you up and takes you
to a clinic

B
A few days later

Your consultation on the
phone had been brief
You'd rattled through the
options and it had hurried
out your mouth
I'd like an abortion as soon as
possible

You've been going over and
over the pitch as if it might be
able to tell you what to do
Your usual habit of burying
yourself in work until your
problems go away
When you got home Joe had
left a note on the table
Staying with Josh for a few days
You don't know who Josh is but
you know that he's a prick
You'd been putting off calling
Joe but you can't wait any
longer
You take a deep breath and
hit his number
Hi how are you
Yeah
How are you
I'm pregnant
You thought there might be
silence
A softening in his chest you
could hold through the phone
But his tone barely changes as
he says without pause
And I presume you are going to
get rid of it?

Your stomach cramps as you
sit in the car and your whole
body feels open and sore

You wonder if you would
have told your dad about
this
You asked him once if he was
sad he didn't have a son *No*
he said
If I had a son he might have had
a chance of being better than me
at football
He said that when you were
on your way to your first
QPR game
The football scarf you'd
begged for suddenly
scratching like a noose
around your neck

You think about Joe giving
you your headphones when
you couldn't sleep
About him saying he
couldn't wait to have
children
How none of it had cost him
anything
You wonder what the words
justice and love mean when
they're put under pressure
How cruel it is when we
arrive at our own
incompatible definitions
I've been offered a job in
Singapore
So I'll come and get my stuff
when you're at work tomorrow
You hang up the phone and
stare at it for a few seconds
before you type abortion
services London

The taxi drops you outside
the clinic
You'd purposely avoided
looking where it was
This is another moment
you're hoping to forget
In the waiting room you try
to catch the faces of the
other women but they sit in
their own worlds
Trapped in their own
thoughts in their own fertility
You sit and wait alongside
them you wouldn't say with
them
You sit in the smells of
bleach and overripe figs stale
coffee and the colder stench
of guilt

You can't find anything clear
you can't work out whether
you need to go to a sexual
health clinic or a GP or a
centre
You're about to give up
when you get a call from
your mum
You pick up automatically
Hey mama you say
My darling girl
She starts nattering about
her new Spanish teacher
You've been trying not to
think about how your mum
was younger than you are
now when she had you
About how many times
you've heard the story

She'd been caught at a
crossroads
On one side a man she'd
fallen for hard
And on the other a job in her
favourite city Barcelona
And then she found out she
was pregnant
She didn't know what to do
for a while
But then she realised you
were a sign
The path was there and the
path was love
But
Uno mas sangria uno mas
A few later and
If I hadn't have got pregnant I
could be living in the sunshine
Your dad wouldn't have ended
things
It had taken you years
before you realised the
problem wasn't you the
problem was he was already
married

When you see the doctor she
asks how you felt when you
found out you were pregnant
Asks how you feel you deal
with difficult situations
If you'd spoken to anyone
about it
How their reactions had
made you feel
About your lifestyle and how
you would imagine a child
would affect that

You say as little as you can
.
.
.
.
.
.
.
.
.
.
.
.
.
.
.
.
.
.
.
.
.
.
.
.
.
.
.
.
.
.
.
.
.
.
.
.
.
.

.

Mum why did you give me Dad's name? You blurt out through the phone
Well he's your father
Is he?
Of course he is
The one time you'd met him he turned up out the blue on your seventh birthday saying he had a gift for you
Your mum was ecstatic before moments later she was ushering you back upstairs
Be a good girl for mummy she whispered as you heard the door lock behind her
I'm sorry she whispered into your hair as you lay half asleep hours later *I just get overwhelmed*
You only opened your eyes when you were sure she'd gone to see a plate of thick white icing next to a half wrapped present and a card from Dad
You'd pressed your finger to the word as if it might be able to tell you something
Mum when you found out you were pregnant did you ever think about – getting rid of it?
Where's all this come from?
Nowhere sorry it's stupid
It crossed my mind

But your dad seemed so happy
he'd always wanted kids and him
and his wife were having
difficulties
I should go sorry –
Okay my darling
I love you
I hope I haven't said the wrong
thing

.
.
.
.
.
.
.
.

The doctor gives you
two pills that you need
to take twenty-four hours
apart
You take the first pill which
contains mifepristone
And you wonder what it
makes you
Pregnant not pregnant half
pregnant
What you are now carrying
The air feels stiff and so you
hum and say
Well that pill really sucked the
life right out of me
The doctor barely looks at
you as she warns that after
the second pill misoprostol
The most common side
effects include abdominal
pain and diarrhoea
And that chunks the size of
lemons might come out
Lemons
These aren't the lemons you
thought life was going to
give you

.

.

Looking out at the future
just like your mother did

You saw your good job and maybe a good husband with a child there too
With its father's piercing blue eyes
But now you feel deluded that vision a nightmare
No one is owed a future they don't deserve
You find a number for a clinic that is about half an hour away from your house
And you call it

.

The taxi is still waiting for you outside
Alright mate you say to the driver
You avoid the photo on his dashboard
A photo of him hugging a smiling child
My daughter he'd said proudly when you'd got into the car
She's very good at maths and winding her mother up
You clutch the codeine you'd tried to refuse
You don't do painkillers don't like to numb your reflexes but she'd pushed them in your hands
The taxi takes you straight to the pitch
You'll only be twenty minutes late for practice
Alex bounds up to you

Alright mate she says *you heard*
Steph's transferring
Barcelona
Your heart feels like it's been
strummed by a hammer
Everything is in your favour
this is yours to lose
Let's crack on shall we
We've got a game to win

On the other end of the line
the consultant is saying
again she needs to hear you
say that you want it
You don't want it you need it
She is understanding but she
says she has to get consent
from you
Have you considered all your
options
You can give us a call back if
that's easier
No I – can I write it down for
you?
I'm sorry I need to hear you say
it
You hang up

You look at the pitch feel the
damp air nestle into your
cheeks like it could call your
face a home
Life exudes from you even
as you shed it
You can do this

You can't do this

Six

A

It's game day

.

You're waiting to get onto
the pitch

.

Since you took the second
pill you haven't stopped
bleeding
It's normal
That's what Dr Jarrett had
said when you told him you
were concerned
You've started wearing
nappies you've found they're
more absorbent than super-
heavy pads
You changed it twice
through the night but it still
got soaked through
You're wearing as many as
you can fit under your kit
At least they've given you a
bit of an ass
Something for the fans

.

.

.

.

.

.

.

.

.

.

.

B

.

It's game day

.

.

You're ready to pitch

.

.

.

.

.

.

.

.

.

.

.

.

.

.

.

.

.

Since you tried that first time
you've called the clinic every
day
Convinced today will be the
day you'll be able to say it
You've been working on the
pitch in every waking
moment
This is the last thing you
have that you can't fuck
up

Your boss had texted you
last night to say she wasn't
feeling great
She'd had her egg collection
and the procedure had been
invasive
And they hadn't managed to
collect anything
Your stomach had instantly
felt rotten
Full of a baby you didn't
want
Eggs you didn't need

You look at yourself in the
changing-room mirror
Your face slips in front of
you as pain sloshes through
your body
You've been on autopilot
since last week
You look down in your hand
three small pills
You guess rules are made to
be broken
You put the codeine in your
mouth
Footballs are the one thing
left you can save
Ready? Alex says to you
Your brothers in?
Yep she rolls her eyes *and
their wives and mum and dad
and some cousins I've never
even heard of before
They're all like oh so women are
actually quite good
Tossers*

You haven't heard from your
mum since you booked her
ticket
You'd sent it to her with the
message *Let me know if you
change your mind lol*
And she'd replied a few
hours later with *See you
Tuesday* and a link to an
article about how France
was running out of butter
As you head out you scan the
crowd
She might not be here
The only other time she saw
you play football was
moments before her life fell
apart
But there she is
And she's wearing a football
jersey
With your number on it
She catches your eye and
does a big thumbs up
Your heart skips a beat

Gary catches you on your
way in
Ever since he'd heard you
were up for promotion
you'd come in to a coffee on
your desk every morning
and yesterday he'd even got
you a cookie
You couldn't bring yourself
to eat it
*Have you heard? Sarah's not
feeling great so I'm going to be
leading the pitch with you*

*She sent me over her notes so I
can just jump in*

.

.

The team lines up and you
head to the goal
Your heart is pounding and
your uterus feels like it's
about to drop out
The ref blows the whistle
And you say to yourself
*Predict the future
But don't anticipate it*

.

.

/ Game time

.

.

.

.

.

.

.

.

.

.

.

.

.

.

.

.

The clients are already here
Gary says
Ready? / Game time
He gestures to the clients
across the room
You've been studying their
photos for weeks but it still
feels odd to see so many
black and brown faces in
your office
Gary is gesturing to you
*This is B she's going to be
leading the pitch with me
today*
With him you thought you
were –
Hands are thrust in your
face for you to shake
Shall we begin?

.

.

.

.

.

.

.

.

Five minutes in and your
eyes have not left the ball
The crowd watching you as
you watch your team
You thought the ball was
safely by the other team's
goal and then you blink and
it's flying towards you

Concentrate
Your coach's words are
regurgitating in your
skull
You are concentrating but
your body is throbbing
Pain is shooting from your
stomach into your hands
You look down and see a
tiny red dot starting to pool
through your shorts
Their striker kicks the ball
and it flies towards you
The pain rises up and you
are blinded by it can't move
can't even see
And the ball rattles past you
into the net
You throw yourself at it even
though you know you're too
late
You've got to at least look
like you tried
1–0
You roar in frustration
Why won't your body play
ball
You use your hands to push
yourself up and the grass
spins
She didn't even fucking try you
hear a man's voice shout
behind you
Even I coulda saved that one
Wanker you shout at him
even though what you mean
is
I'm sorry Mum

Gary is talking about the
company's attitudes towards
financial growth
About how attitudes towards
investing need to change
Diversify
And then he's smiling at the
clients
And then he's smiling at you
You know he's reading your
boss's words but there's
something about the ease
with which he's taken over
The ease with which he
smiled at you
The ease with which he
says
*And we're really excited by what
inside angle
B might be able to offer*

.
.
.
.
.
.
.
.
.
.
.
.
.
.
.
.
.
.
.
.

Your team has picked up
momentum and has
possession
A few near misses
You're desperately willing
them to score to level your
earlier blunder
But then the ball is back by
your goal and the ref blows
his whistle
Handball penalty kick
The other team cheer as
your heart flips in your chest
Not in my goal bitch not
again
Their striker lines up and
you roar making yourself as
big as possible

And as you stretch your
abdomen rips pain sears
through your body
Argghhh you scream
Argghh the crowd roars back

You stand up slowly trying to
stay calm
Trying to push down the
realisation that is filling your
body
There was a time when you
wanted an easy life too
When you looked at the ease
of your boyfriend and you
coveted it
You look at the ocean of
white faces of your team
And the sea of black and
brown faces of the clients
You in the middle like bait
on a hook
The newest member of the
team
The one who was chosen to
bag the pitch
Gary hovers at the back not
even looking at you
Pouring himself a glass of
water slices of lemon and
chunks of ice plopping into
his glass

The ref blows his whistle and
you lock eyes with the striker
Daring her to kick it
You've watched every game
she's ever played she runs
slow and then strikes to the
left

But will she do that today   .
She starts her run up slow   .
and her foot strikes the ball   .
hard and it flies towards the   .
goal   .
And you make a decision   .
and dive to the right   .
You've caught hundreds of   .
balls like this before   .
Trained most of your life to   .
catch things   .
You save you catch that's   .
what you do   .
Today is no different   .
It can't be   .
You will not be someone else   .
who let your mum down   .
The ball is rushing towards   .
you   .
Soaring through the air the   .
sun behind it   .
The outline of it a spot   .
against the sky   .
It looks like   .
It looks like   .

.

.

.   *So here at First Bank we're*
                                passionate about diversifying
                                our portfolio

Hurtling towards you   .
.
                                Over the past few years we've
.   *been consciously scrutinising our*
                                methods

Daring you to catch it   .
.   *We have set up a D&I*
                                department and run regular
.   *training*

You can feel the heat from   .
the crowd eyes piercing you   .

Your skin sore from scrutiny

.

.

.

Save it miss it save it miss it
Catch it drop it catch it drop it

.

.

.

.

.

.

.

.

.

.

.

.

You don't even feel the pain
Your body goes into motion
You hear the crowd roar
And
You've caught it

.

.

.

.

.

.

.

.

.

.

.

.

.

You read in autopilot you
can't bear to look up
But we know if we're to create
more meaningful change we
need to diversify our investors
which is why we want to –
Sorry can I just interrupt you
there –
Gary's voice pierces the room
So we've actually got some
concrete data on all of this
I've been working on some
graphs let me show you –
Gary's mouth is still half full
of water as he stands it
almost dribbles out his
mouth
A slice of lemon floating
between ice and tonsils

.

.

.

.

.

Your blood starts to rise
He only undermines you if
you let him
Thanks Gary I was actually
getting to that part
Not to worry
He smiles at the clients and
extracts the half-chewed
lemon rind from his mouth
which he puts on the table in
front of you
I'm sure you want to see some
serious data

And I've actually got – B would
you mind holding these slides for
me?

.

.

.

.

.

.

.

You look down
And between your hands
You're holding
A lemon
You panic and drop it
And the ball rolls into the
goal

.

You have to put down your
index cards to hold the
slides
Moving in autopilot unsure
how to break from the
pattern he's put you in
You watch as one of the
cards slips off the table and
floats to the floor like a petal
Great so now we've got them up
I want to take a moment for us
to focus on this
He steps towards you and
his brown loafers squeak
He steps towards you and
his breath travels too
Meatless lamb leg rubber
bands and raw egg
And as he steps towards you
his foot squidges your fallen
card
And he doesn't even notice
Brown on white
I'm sorry I can't do this
I'm sorry
Gary you're a cunt

.

You watch the ball roll as
time rolls away with it

.

.

Is anyone else seeing this
Is your skin see-through
Does anyone else
understand

You feel the room tear from
the force of your words
Convention unconvention
jostling for authority in the
space
It's yours to take
At least it should be
But the moment you tried
You lost it

Your teammates are looking
at you
Your coach is shaking his
head
Your mum is

You start to tear Gary's slides
into tiny pieces
Not looking anyone in the
eye
They watch it flake to the
floor and you go to leave
Before a last-minute impulse
makes you pick up Gary's
half-chewed lemon
And throw it in his face

You snap back into time and
your body and you look
down to retrieve the ball but
all you can see is
Lemons
Lemons filling up the goal
Lemons writhing in the net
Lemons glistening and
convulsing on the grass
And between your legs

There's
Lemons coming from your
body
Chunks of lemon whole
lemons but these lemons are
thick and dark and clotted
charred lemon carcasses
And even though you've
never seen them before
You know these lemons
Have always known your
body could make lemons
Could make whatever it was
told to
Rupturing into the world
like pirate treasure
Their salt scraping skin
between your legs
Body turning against body
Citric blister
And the smell
The smell invading like rust
boiled mud and sulphur
And you think
Is that what my baby smells
like

And whatever this is
Whatever you pretended
this was
Pretended so desperately
you almost craved it
You can't do this anymore

This is the last thing you
remember before
everything is over

Seven

A	B
·	In the bathroom you look at yourself in the mirror
·	Twenty-eight alone having just called someone a cunt
·	A bit of a cunt yourself
·	And pregnant
·	You don't recognise yourself
·	This is not the person you thought you'd be
·	You look in the mirror and you know you are becoming your mother
·	Even though you look nothing like her
·	Your face is a meeting place between all the
·	people that have come before you and all the
·	mirrors the world has held up to you
·	Yours only in the gaps between things
When you wake up someone is holding your hand	·
And everything looks bright	·
And the first thing you think is	·
Is that my dad's hand	·
Your body in the hospital bed looks far away and like someone else's	·
You hear words swimming	·
Pregnancy remaining in the womb	·
Septic shock	·

Someone is squeezing your
hand and saying your name
and
Your mother's breath is too
close
You can taste her
disappointment
Feel her thoughts through
the skin of your eyes
You are losing yourself
Slipping between mother
and daughter
Neither of those things

.

.

.

.

.

Her baby

.

Your baby

.

Where does you end and
baby begin

.

.

Is it just language

.

Or a feeling
What was baby if not you

.

.

.

.

.

.

.

.

.

.

.

.

.

.

.

.

.

.

.

You reach out your hand
and it moves both away and
towards you
What is in the gap between
you and your reflection?

.

Is it just language

.

Or a feeling

.

.

This face doesn't belong to
you?

.

You and I

.

.

We are all you and I
Split and at once
The same
But maybe you never
recognised yourself
Too young too old too pale
too dark

.
.
.
.
.
.
.

When you wake again you
can hear talking
What happened you say
Did we win
Did I save it
You had to save it
What's the point of being a
goalkeeper if you can't save
things
By the time the ambulance came
you hear a voice say *blood had*
soaked through three nappies
and two pairs of shorts
Did we win you say
Did I save it you say
But all you can see are blank
sorry faces and you know
deep down it would have
been too hard for the team
to recover
.
.
.
.
.
.
.
.
.

You wake and think you are
alone

Your ideal reflection always
eluding you
You're wondering who sold
you this mirror
What have you bought
From your mother and all
the other hunted women
.
.
.
.
.
.
.
.
.
.
.
.
.
.
.
.
.
.
.
.
.

You jump when you hear the
toilet flush
You thought you were alone
You wipe your face and go to
leave
It's because you are not your
mother that you
know what you need to do
now
.
.

You try to sit up but the
daylight gapes around you
Steady on you hear Alex's
voice
Take it easy chief
Alex I didn't realise –
What day is it?
Wednesday she says *does that*
mean anything to you?
No fuck-all
She takes a breath in *fucking*
terrifying isn't it
Bet they told you nothing was
wrong too
Two little pills but the power to
do all that
I couldn't do it those words the
thought of
Products of the pregnancy
remaining in the womb
Preferred to do it the old-
fashioned way you know
forceps and a hex in the forest

You go to leave but you catch
your boss's eye in the mirror
and stop
I thought you were –
I came to give in my notice
I've been thinking about it for a
while actually
I guess kids weren't meant for
me
But I really really wanted them
I'm sorry if I've been hard on
you she says
It's been well – you can imagine
Or maybe you can't
I'm sorry you say

.
.
.
.
.
.
.

You had a? You can't quite
believe what you are
hearing
Alex is nodding *coach said it*
would be better to keep it quiet
I think my career's over you say
to her *coach will never promote*
me now
Maybe if you talk to him –
But you shake your head
that's not how it works
This is women's football you
don't get second chances
Alex hugs you
As she moves you notice she
is holding a piece of paper
What's that?
Oh my kitchen sink got blocked I
was chatting to your mum
outside and she gave me a
recommendation for a plumber
Two actually – Keith Ealing and
Keith Acton
She shows you the names
scribbled on the page
And you notice the looping
Ks
Their similarity to the
birthday cards with your
football lessons every
year

And your voice catches on
your words even
though you thought they
weren't barbed for your tears
I'm sorry I –
It's not even –
I'm pregnant

.
.
.
.
.
.
.
.
.
.
.
.
.
.
.
.
.
.
.
.
.
.
.
.
.
.
.

Looking good kid

Your boss is looking at you
assessing you
It's your stillness that betrays
you
She can smell your hesitation
And you know she's going to
hate you
You who has the audacity to
destroy the life she so
desperately craves
She is looking quietly at her
hands
There would have been a time
where I would have been very
angry with you
But I can't say it you tell her *I*
can't say that I can't go through
with it
Well you're going to have to
learn to
Do not make this decision for
anyone else

You see your mum appear
over Alex's shoulder
And the moment scratches
as you understand
something you think you
always knew
Mum you say
I'm sorry she says
Your dad he was – forgetful
And I couldn't bear to see you
forgotten about
As she takes her place
amongst all the mothers
who've defended a father
I'm sorry you say

Do you hate me?
But then your mum is
hugging you engulfing you
.
.
.
.
.
.
.
.
.
Your face is drenched and
your mum is trying to soak
your tears up through her
fingertips
You she is saying *you are my baby*
Your dad and I waited years for
you
Times when I thought – nearly
– a baby lost before –
.
.
.
.
.
.
.
She pulls away you between
her arms
We won't mention this okay
This this mishap
When you get out of here that
will be it
We don't need to talk about it
.
.
.

.
.
.
I just want an easy life the
words are panicking out of
your mouth
Make my mum proud good job
good husband
She scoffs *well there's nothing*
easy about that
The bathroom lights are
bright and harsh
.
.
.
.
.
.
.
.
.
What do you want? she asks
Because if you know
For me
For every woman that has come
before
For you
You need to damn well do it
.
.
.
.
.
.
.
You look at her
I want a long nap and a pina
colada by the ocean

I want Joe to understand life
isn't the same for me as it is for
him but I don't want to have to
tell him
I want my mum to know her life
isn't a failure
I want Gary to fuck off
Sorry if that's a bit –
and
I want to not be pregnant
anymore

Eight

A

A few days later you are
discharged
Your mum packs up your
stuff and goes ahead of you
to put it in the car
She took the flowers coach
had sent you with a note that
said
We'll talk about next season
Rest up

B

You stand outside the clinic
and you try to feel conviction
You'd received a few texts
from Joe
Pretending to ask how you
were
Once you'd made up your
mind you'd called him and
said *I'm going to have an*
abortion but it's got nothing to
do with you
You don't know what you
expected him to say

But it wasn't
Cool hope it goes well
And you guessed that was it
You'd asked for love and
were given something you
craved into shape
You were born love deprived
But you love this baby foetus
cells whatever it is
Which is why you have to let
it go
You push open the door

As you come out into the
reception you spot a woman
coming in
And for a second you see
your own face
Your own hunched shoulders
The pain of being in your
own body
You know instantly why she's
there
Jones the receptionist calls out
You turn surprised to hear
your name

Jones the receptionist calls
out
It still sounds funny however
many times you hear it the
name of a man you'd barely
met
Only glimpsed at and known
through a half wrapped
birthday present
You don't know why he'd
given you a football but
somehow you thought he
must know you loved it too

.
.
.
.
.
.
.

Years later your mum had
confessed that his wife had
also turned up that day
Taken your dad and your
mum's happiness with her
All while making you look
like the thief

Jones

She stands up and you
realise it wasn't your name
it's hers
But there's something about
her face
You think you would have
liked a sister
She looks so scared
You head towards the car
she doesn't need your easy
words
What she needs is beyond
language

Jones

.
.
.
.
.
.
.
.
.
.
.
.

You're suddenly aware of
another woman hovering by
the door
You are counting the
seconds until you can let
your body relax again
Until it won't feel observed

.
.
.
.
.
.
.
.
.
.
.

Jones

You think of everything
you've held
All the things you held you
didn't need to but felt you
had too
What were you trying to
predict
All those years of
anticipating the worst

.
.
Have you been in yet?

.

.
Okay
They're going to tell you this
thing about lemons
Don't worry
There won't be lemons

.
They're also going to give you
codeine
Take it but don't be surprised if
it fucks you up

.
How many – er

.
It's mainly just fluff
At eight weeks I saw a picture it
just looks like bits of white fluff
You should google it
It's not all that bloody foetus shit
you see on the posters
Makes you think doesn't it
How many times have we
believed the wrong thing?
If you have any questions about
it I can

.

.
Physically or –

.
All the time
You're making the right decision

.
Oh
Yeah

She turns back and you
think –

.

.
No

.

.

.

.

.
Okay thanks

.

.

.

.
Is it bad?

.
Eight

.

.

.

.

.

.

.

.

.

.
Thanks
When does life begin?

.
I don't know I just

.

.
And you did too

.

.

Thanks

.

I uh –

Life will give you lemons hey

.

.

.

Are you okay?

.

.

May they never come out of your vagina

Postscript

Sixty-five per cent of period tracking apps share data with data brokers and advertisers including Facebook. Facebook has historically given their data to police to aid a criminal investigation. In June 2021, the United States revoked *Roe v. Wade* and at least twelve states have set about the process of making abortion a criminal offence.

It is illegal to donate people's organs after they die without their permission. It is legal to force pregnancy birth and motherhood on those with uteruses.

Abortion is completely illegal in twenty-four countries. These include: Andorra, Malta, El Salvador, Honduras, Senegal, Egypt, the Philippines and Laos. Since 1994, El Salvador, Nicaragua, Poland and the United States are the four countries that have removed or restricted their citizens' right to abortion.

Under the Abortion Act in the UK, someone who is pregnant has to show they would suffer grave permanent injury to their mental health if they did not have an abortion after twenty-four weeks. They have to present themselves as mad, hysterical, unfit or suffering to legally access healthcare.